FOR THE ONES WE'VE LOVED AND LOST

Kimsue, Thunder, Gretchen, Amber, Jabot, Roscoe, Noche, and the pals that touched your lives too.

THE BIG HELLO

Humans don't know how to say "Hi!"
They shake hands, hug, or high five

Us canines use our noses to see what's new
whether its been one day or a few

A quick sniff of a behind
tells me all the info I need to find

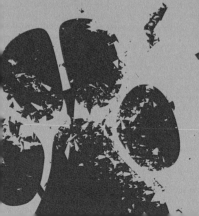

THE LONG GOODBYE

Vets recommend this surgery
I think it's really burglary

As we head to my impending doom
I try to break out of the room

Now bandaged and incomplete
Gone are my days in heat

LOCKED UP

Everyday without fail
you put me in something akin to jail

I spend my day trying to break free
from your terrible tyranny

Hooray for today, I broke down the grate
and now I am free from this effing crate

PRICELESS TREASURE

You follow me here, there, and all around
waiting for me to do my business on the ground

You cheer me on when I'm done
somehow, for you this seems fun

You put it in a bag with such measure
you must think my poop is treasure

THE PRIZE

I might be of small stature and not that tall
what I want is up there, I really want it all

It might be food or something I've never seen
Why hide it up there? That is just mean

When you are not looking I'll get up on that table
You'll be shocked that I was able

BEST FRIEND

Though I can't speak, I can tell how you feel
When you are feeling down, for me it's just as real

I can't tell you that everything will be ok
that tomorrow will be a brand new day

All I can do is curl up with you
and hope that helps while you are feeling blue

DOUBLE DIP

Sometimes what you feed me is so nice
I just HAVE to eat it twice

As I eat I hear you hem and haw
about whether this 'food' should be in my maw

Out one end or the other, you find my meal gross
When I come to give you a kiss, you say adios!

TRUE LOVE

I want to show my affection
A quick look in your direction

I see your leg and it will be mine
You look at me and tell me this is not fine

A quick hump, a few moments of love
then you react with a quick shove

MY STUFF

I can't speak and let folks know what's mine
so I choose to cover them with urine

I takes a quick second for me to pee
why are you cross with me?

I just wanted everyone to understand
that you are MY one and only frand

TASTY TREAT

There are fluffy objects I love to chew
Why does this really upset you

Why do you keep buying pillows in bunches?
You know they serve as my occasional lunches

It gives me much joy from what I just ate
You buy more and stick me in my crate

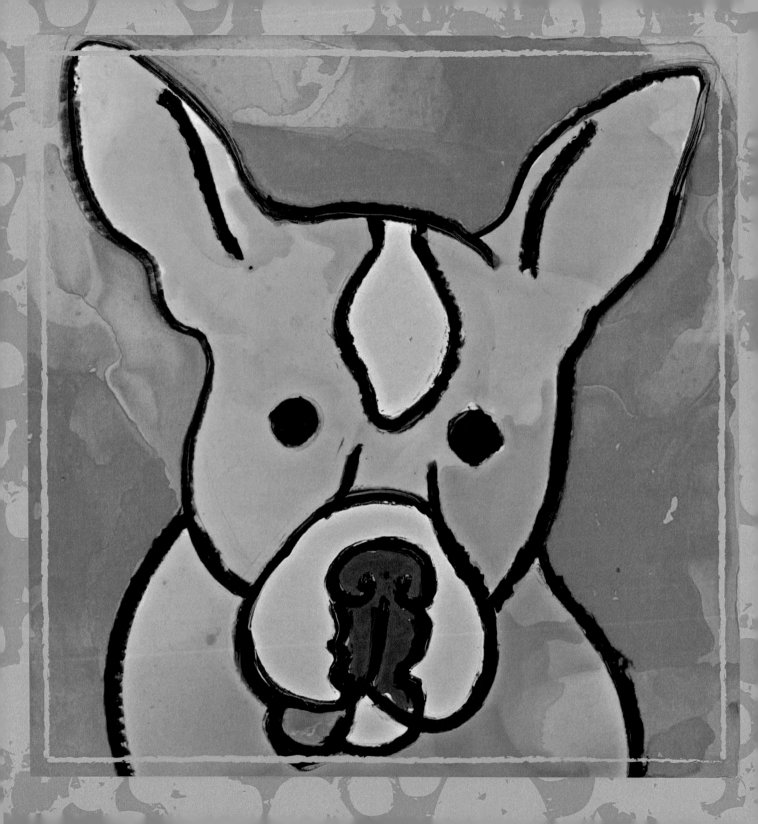

SURPRISE PUDDLE

When I meet new folks I get excited
Sometimes I do something uninvited

I lose control of my bladder
Should that really matter?

Oops, I just peed on the floor
because THEY came through the door!

SUN
SHINE

If you can't seem to find me
just look where its sunny

It feels so nice on my hide
I'll roll over so it hits my other side

I might be underfoot or in your way
this is how I want to spend my day

GAS STATION

Sometimes I act without any class
and the room fills up the smell of noxious gas

Every time you complain as if its something new
God knows you do it too

We should all enjoy this sweet release
and celebrate when I cut the cheese

BOOZE HOUND

I was thirsty, there was your glass on the floor
Now that I had a little, I would like more

I feel a bit funny and the room is spinning
If I could, I would be grinning

I did not know this was risky
I sure did like drinking your whiskey

THE WORST DAY

My time is not measured in decades, just years
Though it is short I live joyously without fear

When I see you I feel nothing but love and light
Our time together makes my existence bright

One day we'll have to say our forever goodbye
I wish I could be there for you, to console you
while you cry

HUG YOUR BEST FRIEND TODAY.

Made in the USA
San Bernardino, CA
14 December 2017